Public Transportation

LET'S TAKE THE
FERRY!

Elisa Peters

PowerKiDS
press

New York

For Julie, in celebration of many trips on the Steamship Authority

Published in 2015 by The Rosen Publishing Group, Inc.
29 East 21st Street, New York, NY 10010

First Edition

Editor: Amelie von Zumbusch
Photo Research: Katie Stryker
Book Design: Andrew Povolny

Photo Credits: Cover James A. Harris/Shutterstock.com; p. 5 Mablache/iStock/Thinkstock; p. 6 Egdigital/iStock/Thinkstock; p. 9 Onepony/iStock/Thinkstock; p. 10 guroldinneden/Shutterstock.com; p. 13 iofoto/Shutterstock.com; p. 14 Philip Lange/Shutterstock.com; p. 17 Boomer Jerritt/All Canada Photos/Getty Images; p. 18 Marcus Clarkson/iStock/Thinkstock; p. 21 George White Location Photography/Photolibrary/Getty Images; p. 22 Dirk Heuer/Flickr/Getty Images.

Publisher's Cataloging Data

Peters, Elisa.
Let's take the ferry! / by Elisa Peters — first edition.
p. cm. — (Public transportation)
Includes index.
ISBN 978-1-4777-6520-3 (library binding) — ISBN 978-1-4777-6531-9 (pbk.) —
ISBN 978-1-4777-6515-9 (6-pack)
1. Ferries — Juvenile literature. I. Peters, Elisa. II. Title.
HE5751.P48 2015
386—d23

Manufactured in the United States of America

CPSIA Compliance Information: Batch #WS14PK4: For Further Information contact Rosen Publishing, New York, New York at 1-800-237-9932

CONTENTS

A **ferry** is a boat. It travels along a set route.

5

Some ferries carry just people. Others carry cars and trucks, too.

The front of a ferry is the **bow**.
The back is the stern.

"Port" means "left" on a ferry.
"Starboard" means "right."

Some ferries are big. Others are smaller.

Ferries can be fast! Their speed is measured in knots.

The crew works on the ferry. The **captain** is the head of the crew.

The Staten Island Ferry is in New York City. It is the busiest US ferry.

A fleet is a group of boats. Washington State has the biggest ferry fleet in the United States.

It is fun to take a ferry. You get great views from the water!

WORDS TO KNOW

bow   captain   ferry

WEBSITES

Due to the changing nature of
Internet links, PowerKids Press has
developed an online list of websites
related to the subject of this book. This
site is updated regularly. Please use
this link to access the list:
www.powerkidslinks.com/putr/ferry/

INDEX